THE JPS B'NAI MITZVAH TORAH COMMENTARY

Re'eh (Deuteronomy 11:26–16:17)
Haftarah (Isaiah 54:11–55:5)

Rabbi Jeffrey K. Salkin

The Jewish Publication Society · Philadelphia
University of Nebraska Press · Lincoln

INTRODUCTION

News flash: the most important thing about becoming bar or bat mitzvah isn't the party. Nor is it the presents. Nor even being able to celebrate with your family and friends—as wonderful as those things are. Nor is it even standing before the congregation and reading the prayers of the liturgy—as important as that is.

No, the most important thing about becoming bar or bat mitzvah is sharing Torah with the congregation. And why is that? Because of all Jewish skills, that is the most important one.

Here is what is true about rites of passage: you can tell what a culture values by the tasks it asks its young people to perform on their way to maturity. In American culture, you become responsible for driving, responsible for voting, and yes, responsible for drinking responsibly.

In some cultures, the rite of passage toward maturity includes some kind of trial, or a test of strength. Sometimes, it is a kind of "outward bound" camping adventure. Among the Maasai tribe in Africa, it is traditional for a young person to hunt and kill a lion. In some Hispanic cultures, fifteen year-old girls celebrate the *quinceañera*, which marks their entrance into maturity.

What is Judaism's way of marking maturity? It combines both of these rites of passage: *responsibility* and *test*. You show that you are on your way to becoming a *responsible* Jewish adult through a public *test* of strength and knowledge—reading or chanting Torah, and then teaching it to the congregation.

This is the most important Jewish ritual mitzvah (commandment), and that is how you demonstrate that you are, truly, bar or bat mitzvah—old enough to be responsible for the mitzvot.

What Is Torah?

So, what exactly is the Torah? You probably know this already, but let's review.

The Torah (teaching) consists of "the five books of Moses," sometimes also called the *chumash* (from the Hebrew word *chameish,* which means "five"), or, sometimes, the Greek word Pentateuch (which means "the five teachings").

Here are the five books of the Torah, with their common names and their Hebrew names.

> **Genesis (The beginning), which in Hebrew is Bere'shit (from the first words—"When God began to create").** Bere'shit spans the years from Creation to Joseph's death in Egypt. Many of the Bible's best stories are in Genesis: the creation story itself; Adam and Eve in the Garden of Eden; Cain and Abel; Noah and the Flood; and the tales of the Patriarchs and Matriarchs, Abraham, Isaac, Jacob, Sarah, Rebekah, Rachel, and Leah. It also includes one of the greatest pieces of world literature, the story of Joseph, which is actually the oldest complete novel in history, comprising more than one-quarter of all Genesis.

> **Exodus (Getting out), which in Hebrew is Shemot (These are the names).** Exodus begins with the story of the Israelite slavery in Egypt. It then moves to the rise of Moses as a leader, and the Israelites' liberation from slavery. After the Israelites leave Egypt, they experience the miracle of the parting of the Sea of Reeds (or "Red Sea"); the giving of the Ten Commandments at Mount Sinai; the idolatry of the Golden Calf; and the design and construction of the Tabernacle and of the ark for the original tablets of the law, which our ancestors carried with them in the desert. Exodus also includes various ethical and civil laws, such as "You shall not wrong a stranger or oppress him, for you were strangers in the land of Egypt" (22:20).

> **Leviticus (about the Levites), or, in Hebrew, Va-yikra' (And God called).** It goes into great detail about the kinds of sacrifices that the ancient Israelites brought as offerings; the laws of ritual purity; the animals that were permitted and forbidden for eating (the beginnings of the tradition of kashrut, the Jewish dietary laws); the diagnosis of various skin diseases; the ethical laws of holiness; the ritual calendar of the Jewish year; and various agricultural laws concerning the treatment of the Land of Israel. Leviticus is basically the manual of ancient Judaism.

➤ Numbers (because the book begins with the census of the Israelites), or, in Hebrew, Be-midbar (In the wilderness). The book describes the forty years of wandering in the wilderness and the various rebellions against Moses. The constant theme: "Egypt wasn't so bad. Maybe we should go back." The greatest rebellion against Moses was the negative reports of the spies about the Land of Israel, which discouraged the Israelites from wanting to move forward into the land. For that reason, the "wilderness generation" must die off before a new generation can come into maturity and finish the journey.

➤ Deuteronomy (The repetition of the laws of the Torah), or, in Hebrew, Devarim (The words). The final book of the Torah is, essentially, Moses's farewell address to the Israelites as they prepare to enter the Land of Israel. Here we find various laws that had been previously taught, though sometimes with different wording. Much of Deuteronomy contains laws that will be important to the Israelites as they enter the Land of Israel—laws concerning the establishment of a monarchy and the ethics of warfare. Perhaps the most famous passage from Deuteronomy contains the *Shema,* the declaration of God's unity and uniqueness, and the *Ve-ahavta,* which follows it. Deuteronomy ends with the death of Moses on Mount Nebo as he looks across the Jordan Valley into the land that he will not enter.

Jews read the Torah in sequence—starting with Bere'shit right after Simchat Torah in the autumn, and then finishing Devarim on the following Simchat Torah. Each Torah portion is called a parashah (division; sometimes called a *sidrah,* a place in the order of the Torah reading). The stories go around in a full circle, reminding us that we can always gain more insights and more wisdom from the Torah. This means that if you don't "get" the meaning this year, don't worry—it will come around again.

And What Else? The Haftarah

We read or chant the Torah from the Torah scroll—the most sacred thing that a Jewish community has in its possession. The Torah is written without vowels, and the ability to read it and chant it is part of the challenge and the test.

But there is more to the synagogue reading. Every Torah reading has an accompanying haftarah reading. Haftarah means "conclusion," because there was once a time when the service actually ended with that reading. Some scholars believe that the reading of the haftarah originated at a time when non-Jewish authorities outlawed the reading of the Torah, and the Jews read the haftarah sections instead. In fact, in some synagogues, young people who become bar or bat mitzvah read very little Torah and instead read the entire haftarah portion.

The haftarah portion comes from the Nevi'im, the prophetic books, which are the second part of the Jewish Bible. It is either read or chanted from a Hebrew Bible, or maybe from a booklet or a photocopy.

The ancient sages chose the haftarah passages because their themes reminded them of the words or stories in the Torah text. Sometimes, they chose *haftarah* with special themes in honor of a festival or an upcoming festival.

Not all books in the prophetic section of the Hebrew Bible consist of prophecy. Several are historical. For example:

The book of Joshua tells the story of the conquest and settlement of Israel.

The book of Judges speaks of the period of early tribal rulers who would rise to power, usually for the purpose of uniting the tribes in war against their enemies. Some of these leaders are famous: Deborah, the great prophetess and military leader, and Samson, the biblical strong man.

The books of Samuel start with Samuel, the last judge, and then move to the creation of the Israelite monarchy under Saul and David (approximately 1000 BCE).

The books of Kings tell of the death of King David, the rise of King Solomon, and how the Israelite kingdom split into the Northern Kingdom of Israel and the Southern Kingdom of Judah (approximately 900 BCE).

And then there are the books of the prophets, those spokesmen for God whose words fired the Jewish conscience. Their names are immortal: Isaiah, Jeremiah, Ezekiel, Amos, Hosea, among others.

Someone once said: "There is no evidence of a biblical prophet ever being invited back a second time for dinner." Why? Because the prophets were tough. They had no patience for injustice, apathy, or hypocrisy. No one escaped their criticisms. Here's what they taught:

> God commands the Jews to behave decently toward one another. In fact, God cares more about basic ethics and decency than about ritual behavior.
> God chose the Jews *not* for special privileges, but for special duties to humanity.
> As bad as the Jews sometimes were, there was always the possibility that they would improve their behavior.
> As bad as things might be now, it will not always be that way. Someday, there will be universal justice and peace. Human history is moving forward toward an ultimate conclusion that some call the Messianic Age: a time of universal peace and prosperity for the Jewish people and for all the people of the world.

Your Mission—To Teach Torah to the Congregation

On the day when you become bar or bat mitzvah, you will be reading, or chanting, Torah—in Hebrew. You will be reading, or chanting, the haftarah—in Hebrew. That is the major skill that publicly marks the becoming of bar or bat mitzvah. But, perhaps even more important than that, you need to be able to teach something about the Torah portion, and perhaps the haftarah as well.

And that is where this book comes in. It will be a very valuable resource for you, and your family, in the b'nai mitzvah process.

Here is what you will find in it:

> A brief **summary** of every Torah portion. This is a basic overview of the portion; and, while it might not refer to everything in the Torah portion, it will explain its most important aspects.
> A list of the **major ideas** in the Torah portion. The purpose: to make the Torah portion real, in ways that we can relate to. Every Torah portion contains unique ideas, and when you put all

of those ideas together, you actually come up with a list of Judaism's most important ideas.

> Two *divrei Torah* ("words of Torah," or "sermonettes") for each portion. These *divrei Torah* explain significant aspects of the Torah portion in accessible, reader-friendly language. Each *devar Torah* contains references to **traditional** Jewish sources (those that were written before the modern era), as well as **modern** sources and quotes. We have searched, far and wide, to find sources that are unusual, interesting, and not just the "same old stuff" that many people already know about the Torah portion. Why did we include these minisermons in the volume? Not because we want you to simply copy those sermons and pass them off as your own (that would be cheating), though you are free to quote from them. We included them so that you can see what is possible—how you can try to make meaning for yourself out of the words of Torah.

> **Connections:** This is perhaps the most valuable part. It's a list of questions that you can ask yourself, or that others might help you think about—any of which can lead to the creation of your *devar Torah*.

Note: you don't have to like everything that's in a particular Torah portion. Some aren't that loveable. Some are hard to understand; some are about religious practices that people today might find confusing, and even offensive; some contain ideas that we might find totally outmoded.

But this doesn't have to get in the way. After all, most kids spend a lot of time thinking about stories that contain ideas that modern people would find totally bizarre. Any good medieval fantasy story falls into that category.

And we also believe that, if you spend just a little bit of time with those texts, you can begin to understand what the author was trying to say.

This volume goes one step further. Sometimes, the haftarah comes off as a second thought, and no one really thinks about it. We have tried to solve that problem by including a **summary** of each haftarah, and then a mini-sermon on the haftarah. This will help you learn how these sacred words are relevant to today's world, and even to your own life.

All Bible quotations come from the NJPS translation, which is found in the many different editions of the JPS TANAKH; in the Conservative movement's *Etz Hayim: Torah and Commentary;* in the Reform movement's *Torah: A Modern Commentary;* and in other Bible commentaries and study guides.

How Do I Write a *Devar Torah?*

It really is easier than it looks.

There are many ways of thinking about the *devar Torah*. It is, of course, a short sermon on the meaning of the Torah (and, perhaps, the haftarah) portion. It might even be helpful to think of the *devar Torah* as a "book report" on the portion itself.

The most important thing you can know about this sacred task is: *Learn* the words. *Love* the words. Teach people what it could mean to *live* the words.

Here's a basic outline for a *devar Torah:*

"My Torah portion is (name of portion) _____,
    from the book of _____, chapter

_____.

"In my Torah portion, we learn that _____
    (Summary of portion)
"For me, the most important lesson of this Torah portion is (what
    is the best thing in the portion? Take the portion as a whole;
    your *devar Torah* does not have to be only, or specifically, on the
    verses that you are reading).
"As I learned my Torah portion, I found myself wondering:
> ➤ *Raise a question that the Torah portion itself raises.*
> ➤ *"Pick a fight"* with the portion. Argue with it.
> ➤ *Answer a question* that is listed in the "Connections" section of
>   each Torah portion.
> ➤ *Suggest a question to your rabbi* that you would want the rabbi
>   to answer in his or her own *devar Torah* or sermon.

"I have lived the values of the Torah by _____
(here, you can talk about how the Torah portion relates to your
own life. If you have done a mitzvah project, you can talk about
that here).

How To Keep It from Being Boring
(and You from Being Bored)

Some people just don't like giving traditional speeches. From our per-
spective, that's really okay. Perhaps you can teach Torah in a different
way—one that makes sense to you.

> Write an "open letter" to one of the characters in your Torah por-
  tion. "Dear Abraham: I hope that your trip to Canaan was not too
  hard . . ." "Dear Moses: Were you afraid when you got the Ten
  Commandments on Mount Sinai? I sure would have been . . ."
> Write a news story about what happens. Imagine yourself to
  be a television or news reporter. "Residents of neighboring cities were horrified yesterday as the wicked cities of Sodom and
  Gomorrah were burned to the ground. Some say that God was
  responsible . . ."
> Write an imaginary interview with a character in your Torah portion.
> Tell the story from the point of view of another character, or a mi-
  nor character, in the story. For instance, tell the story of the Gar-
  den of Eden from the point of view of the serpent. Or the story
  of the Binding of Isaac from the point of view of the ram, which
  was substituted for Isaac as a sacrifice. Or perhaps the story of
  the sale of Joseph from the point of view of his coat, which was
  stripped off him and dipped in a goat's blood.
> Write a poem about your Torah portion.
> Write a song about your Torah portion.
> Write a play about your Torah portion, and have some friends act
  it out with you.
> Create a piece of artwork about your Torah portion.

The bottom line is: Make this a joyful experience. Yes—it could
even be fun.

The Very Last Thing You Need to Know at This Point

The Torah scroll is written without vowels. Why? Don't *sofrim* (Torah scribes) know the vowels?

Of course they do.

So, why do they leave the vowels out?

One reason is that the Torah came into existence at a time when sages were still arguing about the proper vowels, and the proper pronunciation.

But here is another reason: The Torah text, as we have it today, and as it sits in the scroll, is actually *an unfinished work.* Think of it: the words are just sitting there. Because they have no vowels, it is as if they have no voice.

When we read the Torah publicly, we give voice to the ancient words. And when we find meaning in those ancient words, and we talk about those meanings, those words jump to life. They enter our lives. They make our world deeper and better.

Mazal tov to you, and your family. This is your journey toward Jewish maturity. Love it.

THE TORAH

❖ Re'eh: Deuteronomy 11:26–16:17

Re'eh continues Moses's second farewell address to the Israelites. It begins by reminding them that they can choose blessing or curse: a blessing if they obey God's commandments, and a curse if they disobey. The parashah continues one of Deuteronomy's major themes—the prohibition of idolatry—and, for the first time, tells the Israelites that they will have to confine all their sacrificial offerings to one specific place. As Jewish history continues to unfold, the Israelites will understand this place to be Jerusalem.

The portion repeats the basic laws of kashrut, by describing which animals can be eaten and which are prohibited. The Israelites are warned not to follow false prophets, and are instructed to observe the three pilgrimage festivals: Pesach, Shavuot, and Sukkot. And it ends with social legislation: property must be shared with Levites, strangers, orphans, and widows.

Summary

> Moses tells the Israelites that they will always have the ability to decide for themselves between blessings and curses. When they enter the Land of Israel, the tribes will pronounce the blessings on Mount Gerizim and the curses on Mount Ebal, which are opposite each other. (11:26–3)

> He also tells them that when they enter the Land of Israel, they will no longer be permitted to offer sacrifices at just any convenient site. They will worship God only at the place where God chooses. (12:4–16)

> Moses expands the "menu options" for the Israelites. Even though they will have to bring their sacrificial offerings to one specific place, they will still be permitted to eat meat anywhere, as long as they do not eat the blood along with the meat. (12:20–28)

> There is a list of animals that are permitted and those that are forbidden. We find a similar list in Leviticus 11, but there are some significant additions in this version. Here, the list of permitted and forbidden animals comes after very specific prohibitions of idolatry. Further, while the Israelites are not allowed to eat anything that has died a natural death, the text specifies that such meat can be given to the stranger to eat. (14:4–21)

> Moses reviews how people are to share their harvest and treat the poor. The remission of debts and indentured servitude is discussed, against the backdrop that poverty will always be with us. The description of the three important festivals notes that everyone in society should be included in their observance. (14:22–16:17)

The Big Ideas

> **The ability to make moral choices is one of Judaism's greatest gifts to the world.** This is one of the most important differences between human beings and animals. Animals will always act based on instinct; people have the ability to think about the consequences of their options and their actions first. It is also one of the many differences between human beings and computers. Computers never choose to do anything; they only perform based on the information that people enter into them. The ability to choose the good is what has created the civilization we have today.

> **Judaism believes that certain places are holy.** While Judaism has always cared more about sacred *times,* like Shabbat and the festivals, it has hardly ignored the idea that places can be holy as well. Deuteronomy introduces this notion by stating that the Israelites will only be permitted to offer sacrifices at a specific place—which later will be the Temple in Jerusalem.

> **Life is sacred.** This is the main reason why Israelites were not permitted to eat the blood with their meat—because blood symbolizes life. This still forms the basis of kosher slaughtering. The animal must be slaughtered in a particularly humane way so as to minimize pain to the animal, and all blood must be drained from the meat before it can be declared kosher. Some would say that God would have preferred for human beings to be vegetarians, but God understood that this was a rather lofty goal. So, yes, we can eat meat, but it has restrictions attached to it.

> **To be a Jew means to be different.** In Deuteronomy, this seems to be the major reason why certain animals can be eaten and others are prohibited. Differentiating Jews from others was not part of the message the last time this list was presented (Leviticus 11). God is telling the Israelites that when they enter the Land of Israel they will have to learn to continue to exert their differences from the native Canaanites in every way—no worshiping idols, not even tolerating anyone who worships idols, and eating differently. That is still a major reason why many Jews observe the tradition of kashrut; it constantly reminds them of their Jewish identity.

Divrei Torah

IT'S YOUR CHOICE, SO CHOOSE WISELY!

If you have been paying attention for the last few years, you will have heard a phrase that gets thrown around a lot: "pro-choice." It means that a woman can choose her own health options, particularly whether she wants to bear and give birth to a baby.

So, here is what you need to know: *Judaism is pro-choice,* in the broad sense of the term. Judaism is filled with the language of *choice.* God chose the Jewish people to do the mitzvot. The Hebrew word for "young person" is *bachur* or *bachurah*—one who can make choices—which is the whole meaning of bar and bat mitzvah: old enough to choose wisely.

That's what makes the opening words of our Torah portion so powerful. God sets before us blessing and curse. What does that mean? Here, "blessing" means material prosperity; if you follow the mitzvot, you (not "you" as an individual; "you" as the entire People of Israel) will have prosperity in the land. But if you don't follow the mitzvot, you get the curse—which means, frankly, disaster.

God is saying: "There are options in life. There are alternatives. You make the choice." God is like a parent who is dealing with a child who is maturing. "You can choose: do your homework and succeed in school, or don't and you won't be able to take advantage of all the learning that school offers you." God, like a wise parent, cannot force us to do anything, but God wants us to know the consequences of our actions.

That's what makes us human. Rabbi Harold Kushner writes: "The distinguishing characteristic of human beings, setting us apart from other animals, is our ability to choose the values by which we live. Other animals are driven by instinct. Human beings have the potential to control instinct." We train our pets to do certain things, and *not* to do certain things. When they obey us, it is not out of their free will; they have simply trained their instincts so that they earn a reward. "Good dog!" does not mean that the dog is morally good; it simply means that the dog has done what we have trained him or her to do.

It goes even further than that. In one sense, this whole notion of free choice explains why there is evil in the world. The great medieval sage Maimonides totally understood this. "All people have the freedom of choice—to either follow God's laws, or not to follow those laws. Only man, with his knowledge and thought, can distinguish good from evil and choose between the two, and no one can stay his hand from doing good or evil."

According to this view, there is evil in the world as a consequence of God giving us free will. We are free to choose to do good or evil. God hopes that we will choose the good, but God cannot force us to do so. God chooses to limit God's own interference with human nature. That is the wonder, and the peril, of free will.

Some say that God gives us our freedom, but when we abuse it God goes to a secret place and cries. Because of what we are doing to ourselves and to each other—and because God has freely chosen not to interfere.

It is a tough choice . . . for God and for us. So the choice is ours, to choose, and to do so wisely.

THIS MUST BE THE PLACE!

"Why do I need to go to a synagogue? I can pray anywhere!" You might have heard people say that. The same people would never say: "I can play baseball anywhere!" (Because, actually, you can't; you need four bases and an outfield.)

This is one of the great themes of Deuteronomy: now that we are about to enter the Land of Israel, we need some rules, people! One God. No idols or false gods. (Deuteronomy goes ballistic on this issue: don't serve other gods; destroy the places where false gods were worshiped; don't even ask how the other groups of people served their gods!) No local prophets with false messages! And there can be only one place where you serve God. You can't make your offerings at your local "sacrifice places" anymore. No—God will choose a place where God's Name will dwell (which, in ancient times, actually meant where God would live).

That particular place for God winds up being the Temple in Jerusalem, even though the text doesn't say this. Many scholars believe that this "one holy place" order in Deuteronomy actually comes from a much later time, when King Josiah decided to get rid of local sacri-

ficial altars and centralize everything in Jerusalem, and ordered the
people to come to the Temple in Jerusalem on the three festivals—
Pesach, Shavuot, and Sukkot. A midrash teaches: "The world is like
a human eye. The white of the eye is like the ocean. The pupil is the
Land of Israel. The opening of the pupil is like Jerusalem. The reflec-
tion in the eye is like the ancient Temple." That is how sacred Jerusalem has been to the Jewish people.

So, in later biblical times, there was only one place for sacrifice—
the Temple in Jerusalem. And you had to make a pilgrimage there on
the festivals three times a year. That was it? That was all you had to
do to fulfill your religious duties? The pilgrimage was a big deal, but
what about the rest of the year?

Contemporary scholar Jeffrey Tigay helps us with this question.
"Deuteronomy must have expected that some other religious activi-
ties would take the place of sacrifice during the rest of the year. It is
likely that prayer and study were expected to fill the gap."

After the Babylonians destroyed the First Temple in 587 BCE, the
Jews needed another way of serving God. Perhaps that led to the in-
vention of the synagogue—a place of gathering, study, and prayer.
Perhaps the synagogue developed because not everyone could make
the trip to Jerusalem, and they stayed home and prayed and studied.

Now, there is no longer one place where God has chosen for the
Divine Name to dwell. There are many places. Certainly the synagogue is a very important one. An individual may pray and study al-
most anywhere, but a community needs a gathering place. That is why
the synagogue is called *Beit ha-Tefillah* (the House of prayer), *Beit ha-
Midrash* (the House of study), and *Beit ha-Knesset* (the House of gathering). And that is why the synagogue has been the center of Jewish
life for two thousand years.

Connections

> What are some of the most important choices that you have made? Important choices that will affect your future? Your Jewish choices?

> Why has the Land of Israel been considered holy by Jews? What other places in your life are holy? How do you define "holy"?

> Do you believe that Jews should distinguish themselves through what they eat? How?

> Do you believe that it's OKAY to eat meat? In what ways does Judaism protect the dignity of animals?

THE HAFTARAH

❖ Re'eh: Isaiah 54:11–55:5

(Reader note: this haftarah is the same as the haftarah
for Parashat Noah, in the book of Genesis.)

The Jews are now preparing themselves, spiritually, to return to the
Land of Israel. Even still, they need assurances from God, for the
people see themselves as a boat that is being tossed around in a ter-
rible storm (54:11).

But the storm will someday end, and the "boat," which is the Jewish people, will come to a safe harbor. It will not only be a geograph-
ical homecoming, to the Land of Israel, but a spiritual one as well. It
will require that Jews make a renewed commitment to being a people
concerned with *tzedakah*—charity and acts of social justice.

While it seems that God had hidden the Divine Presence from the
Jewish people, and had even sent them into exile in Babylon, in real-
ity, God has never withdrawn love from them.

Are You Making Peace?

I bet you never thought that studying Torah and its varying perspec-
tives leads to peacemaking. It's an amazing lesson—and it is one that
Judaism has tried to teach the world.

Second Isaiah envisioned a time of restoration for the Jewish people, not only physically to the Land of Israel, but spiritually to a state
of peace and happiness. We all have a role in bringing that about, but
need to know how, which is one reason why Judaism puts such an
emphasis on education.

Quick: why do you attend religious school? To learn about Judaism? To learn the history of the Jewish people? To learn Hebrew—or,
at least, enough Hebrew for your bar or bat mitzvah ceremony? To be
with friends? Because your parents say so?

Those are all decent answers. But here's one that maybe you've never
considered: to learn how to think. Jewish education is great prepara-

tion for how to think like an adult. When many people discuss controversial subjects, they can get very worked up, not really listening to their opponents' views, and seeing them in the worst possible light.

But that is not how Judaism views the world. And we find proof of this in one verse of this week's haftarah: "And all your children shall be disciples of the Lord, and great shall be the happiness [*shalom,* which also means 'peace'] of your children" (54:13).

The study of Torah should lead to peace between Jews who are learning Judaism together. It is written in the Talmud, "Rabbi Eleazar said in the name of Rabbi Chanina: Those who study Torah help to build peace in the world. Do not read *banayikh,* 'your children,' but rather '*bonayikh,*' 'your builders.' Those who learn and teach Torah are the builders of the world."

Builders—not destroyers through cruel and harsh language. The best way that you can build the world is through people learning together. That is why Judaism believes that we should study many different opinions.

Here is one example. Traditional medieval commentaries on the Hebrew Bible have a very interesting page layout. The Bible text is in the middle and commentary, or interpretations of the text, from across the centuries surround it. All those teachers "live together" on the same page, in shalom.

Or, look at the mezuzah on a door. It is slanted. Rashi, the great sage of twelfth-century France, said that the mezuzah should be vertical. His grandson, Rabbeinu Tam, said that it should be horizontal. A generation later, Rabbi Jacob ben Asher said that it should be a little of both; it should be slanted—as a way of keeping shalom.

That is why Rav Kook, the first chief rabbi of prestate Israel, said: "When Torah scholars broaden knowledge and provide new insights, they contribute to the increase of peace." All views, even those that seem contradictory, in fact help reveal knowledge and truth. For this reason, the early sage Rabbi Chanina emphasized that scholars are like builders. A building is erected from all sides, using a variety of materials and skills. So too, the whole truth is constructed from diverse views, opinions, and methods of analysis.

An important lesson—be a student; be a builder, be a peacemaker.

❖ Notes

❖ Notes

CPSIA information can be obtained
at www.ICGtesting.com
Printed in the USA
LVHW091832250319
611761LV00003B/406/P

9 780827 614574